The Illustrated Benny Hill

Even at his suavest,
Benny still looks for
support from the
Hill's Angels.

The Illustrated Benny Hill

Gary Morecambe

Elm Tree Books · London

ELM TREE BOOKS

Published by the Penguin Group
27 Wrights Lane, London W8 5TZ, England
Viking Penguin Inc., 40 West 23rd Street, New York, New York 10010, U.S.A.
Penguin Books Australia Ltd, Ringwood, Victoria, Australia
Penguin Books Canada Ltd, 2801 John Street, Markham, Ontario, Canada L3R IB4
Penguin Books (N.Z.) Ltd, 182–190 Wairau Road, Auckland 10, New Zealand

Penguin Books Ltd, Registered Offices:
Harmondsworth, Middlesex, England

First published in Great Britain 1989 by Elm Tree Books

British Library Cataloguing in Publication Data

Morcambe, Gary, 1956
  The Illustrated Benny Hill
  1. Comedy. Hill, Benny
  I. Title
  791'.092'4

ISBN 0-241-12675-4

Book Design by Norman Reynolds

Printed by Butler & Tanner Ltd
Frome and London

To
Louise and Fiona Webb.
For your courage, humour
and most of all,
friendship.

My thanks to the many people who contributed in some way, however small, to the making of this book, with a special mention to Jack Breckon, Val Lee and Paula Eatough at Thames Euston Road; Philip Jones and Dennis Kirkland, Thames Studios, Teddington Lock; Billy Marsh, Billy Marsh Associates, Denmark Street; Eve Lucas and Maurice Thomas, BBC; Jonathan Stuart, for his patience while training me to use the home computer this book was written on. And especially the man himself – Benny Hill – for giving the project the go-ahead. For, without whom . . .

The author and publishers would like to thank the following for permission to use photographs in this book:

Scope Features dedication page (photographer Brian Moody); Jenny Lee-Wright p. 12, 40, 107; The *Sun* p. 15, 75, 82, 93; BBC p. 19, 20, 28, 29; Hulton Picture Company p. 22, 24, 26, 34, 35, 36, 45; *Eastbourne Gazette & Herald* p. 25; Eve Lucas p. 27; Doug McKenzie/PPS p. 30, 99, 100. All other black and white photos courtesy of Thames Television.

In the colour section:

Transworld Feature Syndicate (UK) Ltd p. 1, 2, 3, 6, 7; Jenny Lee-Wright p. 4; Thames Television p. 5, 8 top picture; Sue Upton p. 8 bottom picture.

INTRODUCTION

HAVING written an illustrated book about my father, the comedian, Eric Morecambe, I became keen to produce further illustrated books on other comedians.

Benny Hill was my first choice, simply because so little is known about the man. He must rate as one of the most successfully private people in the top echelon of the entertainment industry.

Benny, I know, had enormous respect for my father, and it was reciprocated. Occasionally, they would rub shoulders in the corridors and canteen at Thames Television, Teddington Lock. My father, jokingly, never forgave Benny for making it so big worldwide, and would continually rib him about it.

Benny broke a twenty-five year absence from the stage to appear in a London Palladium tribute show, as a mark of respect to my father after his sudden, untimely death.

My mother, Joan Morecambe, being introduced to artistes at the Eric Morecambe London Palladium 'Bring Me Sunshine' tribute show. Prince Philip is shaking hands with Benny. Comedy duo Cannon and Ball look on.

Perhaps I am biased when it comes to Benny, because I know how much he appreciated my father's work. I must say, that one of my first thoughts before contacting him about my idea to write this book, was of the stunning flower arrangement he sent to our local church on the day of my father's funeral. Such spontaneous and generous acts can say much about a person.

It might seem incongruous for the son of a famous comedian to be writing a book about another famous comedian, especially when the two comics have little similarity in style and method of work. But comedy – *all* comedy – has been a major part of my upbringing, and I have discovered that, in the final analysis, there is more common ground between my father and Benny than I initially realised. Not only did they have the same professional attitude towards their work, gaining immense respect from most they came in contact with, they also thrust themselves into each show with the kind of enthusiasm and dedication that is needed if you are to reach the top of the show business tree and remain there.

There are two reasons why I personally am a Benny Hill fan. One is that I only have to see his cheeky grin to laugh, and the other, that I am convinced no-one but Benny himself could do the things he does on screen and be so successful at it.

This book, like *The Illustrated Morecambe,* is not, strictly speaking, a biography: more an illustrated and anecdotal tribute to one of Britain's most remarkable comic talents of all time.

WHEN Alfred Hill was sixteen years old, he ran away from home to join the circus. When the First World War broke out, he joined the army, and his career in the entertainment industry was over.

But history was to repeat itself curiously, then go several stages further. For the younger of his two sons, Alfred Hawthorn Hill – better known these days as Benny Hill – was destined to become one of the most popular entertainers of all time.

A staggering one hundred million viewers world wide tune in to Benny Hill shows. Meeting this quiet, slightly shy man, who has always enjoyed a certain anonymity and love for privacy, you could be forgiven for asking yourself, How? How has he become one of Britain's biggest entertainment exports since Chaplin?

His rise to fame and fortune has hardly been meteoric, his career spanning almost half a century of hard graft. Yet a cheeky grin, a superb use of innuendo matched with perfect comic timing and visual presence, plus an ever-changing repertoire of gorgeous nubile girls – the Hill's Angels – adds up to a self-confessed non-intellectual comedian transformed into a living legend.

A top American producer once said that the only comedians to compare with Benny are Charlie Chaplin and Laurel and Hardy.

Clint Eastwood was one of the first to latch on to Benny Hill mania. He rang up the comic when he was in the States on a rare visit, asking if he could meet him and bring his son along. Eastwood's

Benny on the studio floor during the recording of a show.

restaurant, The Hog's Breath, in Carmel, California, is adorned with photographs of Benny.

Part of his extraordinary popularity in America has been attributed to the sauciness of the routines, notably those revolving around semi-clad girls. But it runs much deeper than that.

Much of America's entertainment history lies in burlesque and vaudeville. This, essentially, is what Benny is about. He has taken this imagery and reproduced it for us on the television screen, and in doing so has perhaps captured a nostalgia that American audiences find they either consciously or unconsciously relate to.

Associated with Benny for many years and, until recently, Head of Light Entertainment for Thames Television, is Philip Jones.

Thames was founded in 1968, and Benny was one of the first top-flight artistes to join them.

'Early on, we were not to know just how remarkable it was all going to be,' explained Philip. 'His shows were considered raunchy, but personally I've never believed them any more outrageous than Mack Sennett's bathing beauties of the nineteen twenties. But when I was over there selling the shows, I was asked if I felt he would upset a portion of the American viewing public. I told them, you always

The early days of Benny with female support. 'I used to watch comedians in shows like "Oo La La" ...' said Benny. '... I used to think how lucky they were, standing there, always surrounded by pretty girls ... [I decided] "That's going to be the life for me one day."'

Jenny Lee-Wright in
one of her many
performances. Here
she is in the hands of
'fireman' Bob Todd.

upset a minority with whatever you show. What we hadn't realised was how great would be the adoration of the majority.'

From a quiet introduction, Benny went on to become an international superstar. Philip can still hardly believe the way things developed.

'We took a week's air time on a TV station in New York – one of RKO's stations – which means we actually bought it so we could put in the whole week's programming as we wanted. One of our first choices happened to be a Benny Hill show. Then the notion came of cutting the one hour shows into two half-hour units for syndication across the States.'

Benny's exposure had so far been limited out there, but Thames had plenty of material to edit into the half-hour units. Success wasn't instantaneous. It was when New York and Los Angeles got good ratings that the others joined in. Quite often now the shows go out twice nightly.

Peter Charlesworth is a theatrical agent and long-time friend of Benny's. He says that Benny was as surprised as everyone else by his enormous overseas triumph.

'In Las Vegas, they show Benny Hill in the lounges during the afternoon. If you get talking to people about him, you soon discover many of them think he's dead. At least, they did until he went out there recently. They can't accept he could be so low-key and un-star-like.'

Actress Jenny Lee-Wright, who first worked with Benny over twenty years ago, had first-hand experience of how much America has taken to him.

'I went over to New York for a holiday,

and just to look at the set-up over there,' she said. 'Within moments of my arrival, I met an agent and happened to mention that I had done work with Benny. Forty-five minutes later I had been taken from the airport to a studio and was answering questions about him on a chat show. I think that was quite some going.'

A fact not so well known about Benny and his American success is that he appeared in two shows out there some time before his own were transmitted. They were in 1967 and '68, in a British and American co-production entitled *Spotlight*. The first of these saw him working with Noel Harrison and Abby Lane, in which he sang totally straight a version of 'New York, New York'. In the second show, he worked with singers Lana Cantrella and Paul Anka. The shows came and went, and no one in America could have guessed what would happen the next time he appeared on their screens in his own shows.

This unpretentious, unlikely hero calls himself a 'People's Comic', and his cuddly appearance and mild manner certainly enhance the image. But there is much, much more to Benny beneath the cheeky façade.

All the accolades were a long way off when he was living in a terraced house in Wilton Road, Southampton, being brought up with an elder brother and younger sister.

He was born on 21 January 1925, in Southampton. His mother was a clerk at Toogoods rolling mills before her marriage, and his father, a surgical appliance outfitter.

Alfred Hill, aged
about seven.

Benny in drag: as
Katie Boyle by a
Eurovision song-
contest scoreboard;
Fanny Craddock
(with Henry McGee
as Johnny) in the
kitchen; and in a
Mary Quant/David
Bailey takeoff.

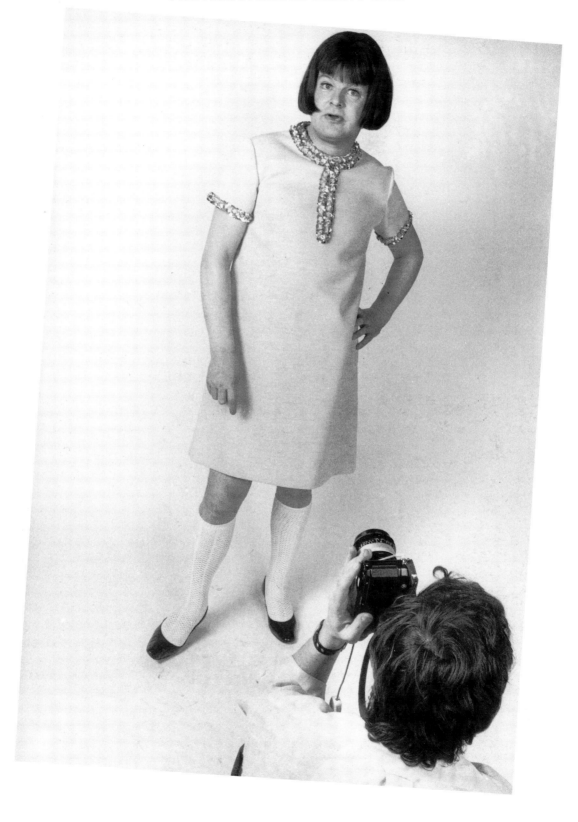

Benny didn't thrive much on schooling. He found academic work boring, and was basically a lazy student. He attended Taunton's School, in Southampton: a boys' grammar catering for some eight hundred students. Future film mogul, Ken Russell, also went to Taunton's, though their years did not coincide.

At the age of fourteen, and while still at school, he became second comic with 'Bobbie's Concert Party'. They were a semi-professional outfit, staging Sunday lunch-time shows in working men's clubs – a standard testing ground for any budding British comic of the era.

He was a regular visitor to the Palace and Hippodrome theatres, and loved the touring revues that the Palace brought in. They were fast and saucy, and full of girls, and had suggestive titles like *Scandals of Broadway*.

Benny's first stage appearance was in a school production of *Alice in Wonderland*. He carried a sign round his neck explaining he was a rabbit, and occasionally uttered appropriate squeaking noises.

But most of his entertaining during the early years was for friends and relatives only. Impressions were his forte, though he was keenly interested in music, an interest that has not left him during his long career.

He ventured out into the world of amateur concert parties, supplementing it by playing the drums for a local band.

His first full-time employment was as a stockroom clerk in the local branch of Woolworth's. He found it a claustrophobic occupation and soon abandoned it to become a milkman. It was while

Early portrait

Benny doing his bit for the country during the war? A sketch from one of his BBC shows.

doing the rounds he began developing a career as an entertainer.

Slightly against parental wishes, at the age of seventeen, Benny left home, and, accompanied by a cardboard suitcase, set off for the bright lights of London.

He sold his drum kit for six pounds, and had a further two pounds in savings. Things didn't happen immediately on the work front. In fact, he found himself spending his first four nights out in the open, firstly on a patch of grass, then on concrete in an unfinished air-raid shelter.

The following Monday saw some relief. He was offered a three-pounds-a-week job, low down in music hall. Hardly a glamorous start to an illustrious career, but it was his first true introduction to professional entertaining.

He went on to tour the country as a 'feed' until the war, when he eventually joined the REME, having first been arrested by Military Police at the New Theatre, Cardiff: his call-up papers had failed to catch up with him while he was touring.

He was to become a driver/mechanic. Benny describes himself as a lousy mechanic who couldn't put a lavatory chain together. He did so much pressurised driving for the Army, that he later vowed never to drive again, and he never has.

Towards the end of the war, he was happily transferred to Combined Services Entertainment.

Once back as a civvy, he became commonly known as Benny Hill – 'Alf 'Ill' sounded too much like a cockney comic. His army gratuity of fifty pounds had fallen

And the girls begin to
shed clothing . . .

to fifteen shillings before he found work. He started out in variety shows in London, though his real interest began turning towards the new medium of the time – television.

The late forties and early fifties were not his best years. He worked as 'feed' for Reg Varney in Margate summer shows and disliked it. He wasn't regarded by the powers-who-were as likely to succeed as a comedian in his own right. He saw this as a nonsense and soon went his own way.

During the fifties, much of Benny's work was on radio and the stage. Radio included *Educating Archie,* in which he played the supercilious tutor of Archie Andrews.

He featured in two West End revues: *Paris by Night* and *Fine Fettle.* And in 1953 he did a very successful summer season at the Wellington Pier, Great Yarmouth, for impresario Billy Marsh – who was then working with Bernard Delfont – in a co-production with Richard Stone, Benny's agent.

It's interesting to note that in spite of its success, Benny had already numbered his days as a 'live' performer. Benny claims that it was in fact the West End shows that put him off theatre all together. During the summer months he had to contend with an audience comprising mainly foreign visitors, and they were there to look at the girls, not the male comic. This is possibly the reason that his own TV shows went on to be so full of girls.

He tried his hand at comedy scriptwriting, at which he was moderately successful, but being a television star still

A production of *Dick Whittington* at the Devonshire Park Theatre, Eastbourne, c. 1950.

A photocall from the mid '50s.

appealed to him more than anything.

Benny also established himself in a successful BBC-TV show called *Showcase*, was chosen as TV Personality of 1953–4 by readers of the *Evening News* so when, due to being sacked after flopping in Sunderland, he found himself writing comedy material which he showed to Ronnie Waldman, then Head of BBC-TV Light Entertainment, he was not wholly without a track record. Waldman immediately offered him his own show.

Peter Charlesworth first met Benny during the early fifties. Peter was in the process of leaving the music business to set up as a theatrical agent.

'Having had a reasonably lucrative job, it was a bit frightening to make such a move,' he recalled. 'But only one man kept

Benny with Lord and Lady Delfont, at a Variety Artists' dinner.

me going through the six or so months of unemployment, and that was Benny Hill. He was incredibly kind to me. Basically, he gave me work. He doesn't drive, and I had a beaten-up Ford Consul. I drove for him. On a couple of occasions I even stood in as his "straight man", on Sunday concerts. He paid me far more than I was worth, and I was dreadful. But he never said anything.

'It all began with Benny, who is prone to discuss matters in the third person, asking me what I was doing one particular Sunday.

' "Nothing," I answered.

' "Right," he said. "Well, Charlesworth will come with Hill, and they will go to Southend. Charlesworth will drive, Hill will pay for the lunch, Charlesworth will supply car and petrol."

'He was very careful to establish a proper working relationship. It was his way of allowing you to retain your dignity. Really, he didn't need me all that much. But he knew he was probably saving my skin at that time.'

Benny had some tremendous years with the BBC, though he was to leave them, rejoin them, and finally leave them to join Thames.

PA to BBC producer Ken Carter and, later, David Croft, was Eve Lucas. She was witness to Benny's introduction of Fred Scuttle.

'The idea was that the Scuttle character was to take off in a makeshift rocket. There's an explosion, and he re-emerges saying, "Hello, moon!" When the explosion occurred, a fire chief appeared from seemingly nowhere, demanding, "I

Dining with Eve Lucas [on Benny's right]. The man was a friend of his from the medical profession, and the young lady, a girlfriend called Annie. Always keen to keep his private life private, Benny introduced all his girlfriends as Annie.

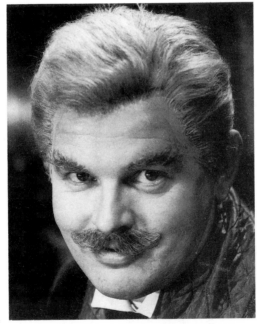

Benny in character roles from his early shows.

want a memo about this. No-one mentioned explosives." There we were trying
to film this routine, and he's going on
about a memo.'

Harold Snoad, an executive producer
who worked with Benny in the early sixties
when just a junior assistant, tells of another
disaster which occurred on location.

'We were filming a "quickie" on
location at Chelsea Bridge. A fee had been
paid for the use of a woman's basement
flat. The routine was that Benny leans out
across a window ledge and then gets
sprayed by a road cleaning machine
coming along. The crew were a little over-
zealous with the water dispensation. Benny
got blasted off the ledge, and the flat was
flooded.

'I can still picture the horrified woman
returning to see the mess, and Benny and
the crew trying to calm her with anxious
promises to clear it all up.'

On another occasion, Benny wanted to
do an impression of Ena Sharples of *Coro-
nation Street* fame in the programme, and
Harold Snoad had to ring up Violet
Carson, the actress who played Ena, to ask
to borrow the authentic overcoat:

'She agreed, but she needed it for a
recording the night before our studio day,
and I remember having to wait at a London
mainline station to collect this precious
garment off a train.'

Someone who made the transition from
channels with him was actor and colleague
Henry McGee, whose face, in conse-
quence, is almost as famous across the
globe as Benny's itself.

'The format for Benny's show is won-

**A man who adores
making music.**

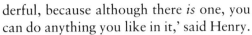

derful, because although there *is* one, you can do anything you like in it,' said Henry.

'The first time I worked with him all those years back, I had quite a fright. I can't exactly pin-point it, but his timing is ever so fractionally different from any other comic's I've worked with. The thing is, you cannot truly tell what a comedian's timing is like until you stand him in front of a live audience.

'We were doing one of our many-to-come sketches that were a major part of the earlier years: just two fellas in conversation of some kind. I was acutely

OPPOSITE: **Among the many accolades Benny has received in the course of his career, the appearance of Fred Scuttle at Madame Tussaud's ranks highly.**

A shot from one of many western scenes. Benny is supported by Henry McGee.

aware in a split second that there was this emphatic difference. And it took me nearly two years to become absolutely *au fait* with his style. There were more words in the shows during this period. This was prior to the universal interest he now receives, that dictates that the shows need to be more visual in content.'

In 1969, Benny was made ITV Personality of the Year. That same year his show was entered for the Montreux Festival. In 1971, his shows received the SFTA's Light Entertainment Award, for Pro-

Being honoured by the Variety Club of Great Britain, in 1965. With Benny are Dorothy Tutin and Ken Dodd.

duction and Direction, as well as the CRAFT Award for Best Script.

'He's always done no more than two or three shows a year for us,' explained Philip Jones. 'I used to offer him guest appearances and so on, mainly to keep him in the public eye in between times. Gently and patiently he would refuse. Then one day I asked him again if he'd like to do an appearance on something, and he said, "The fact is, if I restrict my appearances the shows become more of an event for the public." I didn't agree with him at the time.

A host of famous comic faces gather in conference. Benny is at the far end, left.

**As Professor Peach in
*The Italian Job.***

Years on, I can now see he was perfectly correct. You only have to look as far as his viewing figures to realise that.'

It hadn't always been that way. In April 1955, Benny appeared as a celebrity guest on *Something To Shout About*. In February 1956, he guested on the chat show *Off The Record*. He was interviewed a further twice in 1956 – on *Talk Of Many Things* and *Saturday Night Out*. Another chat show appearance followed in June of 1957 – *Now* – and in 1961, he took part in *Ask Anne*, and that September presented prizes on *Blue Peter*. In March 1962, he was a judge on *Come Dancing*. Then all public and televised appearances outside of his shows apparently ceased.

Benny has appeared in several films including *Those Magnificent Men in their Flying Machines* and *Chitty-Chitty-Bang-Bang*, in which he played the Toymaker. But filmwise, he will be most remembered for his role as Professor Peach – a man obsessed with large ladies' bottoms – in *The Italian Job,* which starred Michael Caine. None of them was anything more than a cameo role, and because Benny's screen appearances were succinct he made sure he gave the audience the best he could in his various roles. He tended to play characters not dissimilar from those that crop up in his TV shows.

He has also found chart success. In the early seventies he brought out a single called *Ernie*, all about a milkman who 'drove the fastest milkcart in the West'. Perhaps a reflection on previous employment!

As much a part of the team these days as

Henry McGee is comic actor Bob Todd.

Bob is an ex-RAF Squadron Leader, turned Sussex farmer, turned entertainer. The entertaining came late in his life, and attaining a role in the *Benny Hill Show* took some dogged persistence.

'I'd long been a fan of the show, and could see myself fitting in with it. So I wrote to the producers again and again, but nothing happened. They couldn't use me. I must have written for months, collecting many polite rejections. Then eventually I accepted defeat. Ironically, the moment I stopped trying, I was booked

Benny with Nicholas Parsons (with the famous big red book) and guest Robertson Hare, in 'Brass bandsman Fred Scuttle, this is your life.'

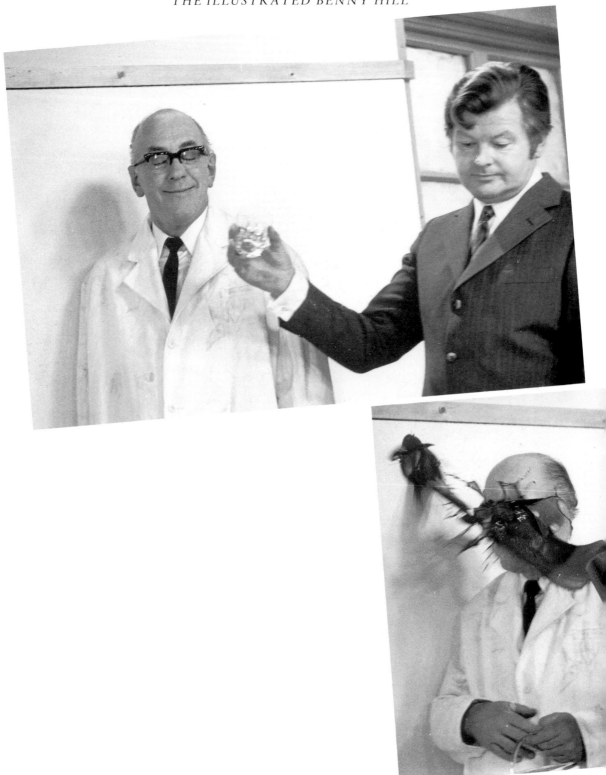

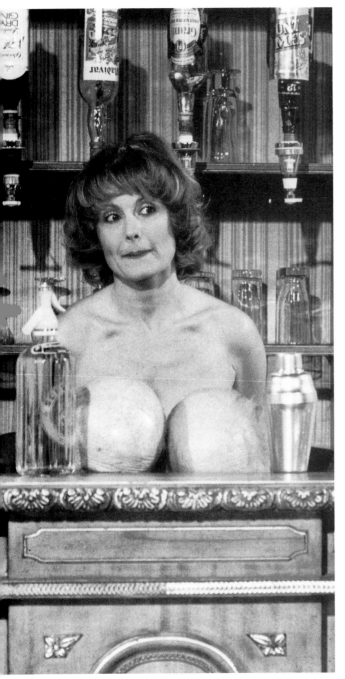

for a part in the next show.'

Sixteen years on, Bob is still going strong. 'We have a fixed relationship. We work hard together, I call him Ben, he calls me Toddy. It's all wonderfully friendly, but I don't impose on him, and he never decries me. With Henry and the others, it's been a lovely team to be associated with.

'I'm not a crawler. I wouldn't write letters to him every week, or try to raise him on the phone just to keep favour with him. Benny can't be tricked. If the show needs you, then you will be used. One day, he may come to think, "Old Toddy's over the hill," and that will be that.'

Bob is a giggler, and at work he sometimes finds it hard to contain himself.

'There was one particular time when Benny and myself were supposed to be German sailors, both speaking mit zee arkcent, ja! We broke up half way through the sketch, and I'm sure it was the first and last time I've ever seen Benny go like that. Afterwards, I could hear him telling everyone with a chuckle, "It's that bloody Bob Todd."'

Nicholas Parsons joined the show out of the blue. He and Benny had appeared in a charity show at The Prince of Wales Theatre, during the sixties.

Nicholas used to be an impersonator, so Benny asked him to play the part of Eamonn Andrews in a spoof he had written of *This Is Your Life*.

'It went extremely well with the live audience,' recalled Nicholas. 'Benny was watching and waiting for his cue in the wings, apparently complaining to whoever was nearest him that I should be pulled off the stage. "Who booked him anyway?" he joked. "He's getting bigger laughs than me." It was that kind of thing.

'Some years later, after I had finished working with the comic Arthur Haynes, Benny resurrected the *This Is Your Life* routine for television, introducing Fred Scuttle who is special guest on the programme and who doesn't know any of the friends and family "Eamonn" is calling on. A very funny idea that worked well, and suddenly I was a regular on the show.'

Benny is not a difficult man to work with, according to his colleagues.

'He has no false illusions about himself,' said Jenny Lee-Wright. 'The shows have a great sense of camaraderie about them. He's the sort of man that may ring up tomorrow saying he has a suitable part for you in the next production. He doesn't forget what your strengths and weaknesses are. He remembers the part you played before almost better than you do.

'When working on a show, he would always pull you up with a joke if you had forgotten your lines, but equally it was easy to tell that he very much wanted you to know them – to get them exactly right. You do have to know what you're doing when working for Benny. Sometimes, if I was having difficulty with a certain line or two, I could go up to him and let him know, and he would be brilliant and constructive in his advice and assistance. And when things didn't go well on a show, I often felt it created a nagging problem in Benny's mind. "Is it me? the script? or the people I've chosen?" You could nearly hear him thinking these thoughts.'

OPPOSITE: **Jackie Wright and Bob Todd give a fresh meaning to the term 'supporting actors'. Jenny Lee-Wright is the one getting the support.**

OVERLEAF: **Benny being intimidated by forthright girls.**

Philip Jones pointed out, 'He is a great professional. Whatever your formula, you don't sustain such acclaim by good fortune alone. He has an instinctive knowledge of pace. He can tell the moment he sees something whether it has worked or not. For example, a lot of the "quickies" and sketches he does are pre-recorded, then shown to a studio audience. After the recording, a play-back session at once follows for artistes, producer and so forth, on the studio monitors. More than once I have seen him watch himself, then say, "Let's just do it one more time. They'll have all gone home." By that, he means the pace is too slow. The audience will have figuratively, if not literally, switched off before the punch-line's been delivered.'

In 1984, *The Benny Hill Show* won the comedy prize at the Montreux Festival. And now, at sixty-four years of age, Benny shows no sign of retiring, and will undoubtedly continue to collect awards as he strives ever forwards.

For many years, Benny lived in Queensgate, near Knightsbridge, London. Now, albeit temporarily, he has returned to his Southampton roots, maintaining the modest home he once bought for his parents. He intends returning to south-west London in the near future, for the convenience of being near the television studios that record his shows.

A new home in Queensgate, London.

Benny flanked by
Thames 'big boys', his
producer, Dennis
Kirkland (left) and
then Head of Light
Entertainment, Philip
Jones. They are
celebrating the
comic's sixtieth
birthday party aboard
the Thames boat at
Teddington Lock.

*T*HE producer for Benny's Thames Television shows is Dennis Kirkland. Dennis gave me the following run-down as an example of a typical schedule for the making of one Benny Hill show.

Two film scripts arrive in May, which will be used for filming in early September. [Benny likes to keep the summer months clear of work.] Six or seven film scripts will eventually be needed, but two is an acceptable start.

By July/August, all scripts – all written by Benny – should be in Dennis's hands. In the end, they are always left with too much material, but this is all to the good: it gives them something to fall back on if necessary.

The films are scripted and cast by August. Location filming commences in September, and takes three weeks to film for all three shows that Benny makes during any one year. That means all the location filming is done in one three-week session – one week per show. In reality, however, it now means two films per week per show, as the famous run-off sequence to the music 'Yaketty Sax' that closes each show has become a special six-minute slot of its own, extending from the last skit in the show itself. No longer is it just a short gag involving Benny running around a few trees with irate girls, as it used to be.

A month out follows while Dennis edits the film ready for audience consumption. Then it is into rehearsals for a short period, then into the studios for three solid days

Benny in various
guises during location
filming.

of 'quickies' – short routines to be shown to a studio audience along with the film and sketches in the show, at a later date.

Benny has the following week clear to work on any re-writes, and Dennis starts talking dance and musical routines with the girls, and allows Libby Roberts, choreographer, to start working out a few basic ideas with the script as it stands. Benny works with her in closer detail at a later date, though he will have played a major part in deciding what the musical numbers for the show will be.

A week's rehearsal culminates in four consecutive days in the studio doing the major inserts of the girls' dance routines, which Benny is now involved with. He likes to drop in fresh gags, and quite often slightly alters the routines to suit his needs. It is a trial and error period. The final routine eventually shown to a studio audience is quite often not the final routine to be televised. The studio audience see it in a fairly raw state. It is later improved in a master edit.

From the rehearsals, they concentrate on dubbing the music and special effects. This takes about five days.

Now it is edited into a rough-cut for the audience to see. The following week is final rehearsals, leading into the show's recording in front of the studio audience on the Friday night.

On show day, Benny arrives at 9.30 a.m., and his day ends after recording at 10 p.m.

Much of what the audience see is recorded, as much of Benny's show comprises 'quickies' and pre-recorded film. But all the extra bits are done to the audience

Benny is involved in every aspect of the shows.

50

A typical Benny Hill routine, combining his love of uniformed characters with glamorous girls. The sequence was shown at double speed, an essential ingredient of the later, more visual shows.

on that Friday night. He also does an unrecorded warm-up routine with Dennis, and then one of his well-known monologues.

Dennis Kirkland says that it is one of the hardest shows he has ever worked on. 'It's easy to forget that you can shoot a seven-minute sequence that in reality will only run three minutes because of being recorded double-speed to suit Benny's needs. If you were to run his show at normal speed, it would probably run nearly three hours – for a *one* hour show.'

Benny has his own idea of how he sees the show coming together. To choreograph it on that basis is not easy for Libby Roberts, but she copes very well,

Benny likes to make visual gags from words. This is a particularly good example.

and is a strong member of the team.

'You go along with it because that's the way it is,' she said, quite honestly. 'Benny will say, "We're doing *Carmen*," and that will be fine, because it's all there to copy. But on the other hand, he'll approach me saying, "We could do a cabaret routine of some kind. What do *you* think?" He'll leave me to ponder for a while. "Try and

get a little angle on it," he'll add. "Something clever." You see, he can't bear a straightforward dance routine that's used basically as a gap-filler. He likes to think the dance routine has reason to be there. A *raison d'être*, as he calls it. Therefore, comedy and tricks become necessary.'

One of his best tricks came in a tango routine. 'It required him to be shown to walk at quadruple speed, while those around him remained at normal speed. These are the kind of ideas he enjoys working on. He has his specific gags he wants to use, but he will ask me how we can do such-and-such a routine. That's how we work.'

Benny's never happier than when dressed as a clown. In this routine his arms are elongated in a tug-of-war between his girls.

Jackie Wright and Rita Webb in their finest 'rags' for a Benny Hill routine.

Benny, the versatile
musician.

58

Unbelievably, four days of the show's edit goes into sound dubbing and effects. Over the years, and with many laughs in the process, Benny and Dennis have become minor specialists in this field, going to extreme ends to find just the right imitation of a particular sound they require.

'Our sound men, Richard and Clive, who do much of the actual work in the studio, are very quick considering the amount of dubbing that each show needs,' explained Dennis. 'And it has to be right. There is no point someone falling from a wall if they don't hit the ground with a sickening thud. For that is where the laugh is.

'You must remember, if you want to recreate the noise, for instance, of a slamming door, the worst thing you could do is record the sound of a slamming door. It would be quite ineffectual, coming across as a dull click.

'A face slap, which is something used on the show a lot, is lost by recording the slapping of a face. We've discovered that the best face slap is the sound of a popping balloon greatly reduced. It becomes an almighty whack.

'The sound room is a wreck while all this is going on. On my way there to do some dubbing, I inevitably visit the corner shop and buy crunchy apples, carrots and celery. Celery is particularly useful. It's the ultimate sound impression of somebody being kneed in the groin.

'But there is an art to using sound effects. For example, if you are going to tear the dress off a girl, you start tearing before or after the visual move – not concurrently.

This focuses the eye to the point of action.'

Benny himself is brilliant at effects. If he opens something in his kitchen and it makes a catchy sound he hasn't noticed before, he'll make a note of it. One of his latest finds is an empty, plastic Coca-Cola bottle.

'It makes the perfect "ponking" sound,' said Dennis. 'That is, rather than a "thudding" or "ringing" sound. But the studio cleaner took it away one morning before we had tried it out properly. Next day, Benny went out and bought another one, drank the contents, and was ready for action again. Once he has a definite sound in mind, there's little one can do to dissuade him from trying it out.

'Hours are spent trying to achieve these sounds. The dubbing aspect is vital to the success of the show. Every now and then we'll find a classic one, and curl up on the floor in hysterics.'

Affected agony

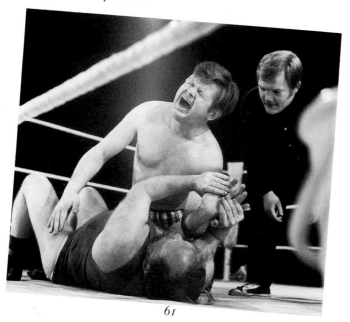

Headmaster Hill with
a favourite pupil

*T*HERE was a ritual to becoming a Benny Hill girl, as Erica Lynley can recall. He used to do all the interviewing in his opulent London flat, sometimes with a group of girls, other times individually. But it was all above board, and very professionally handled.

'There were moments when I first arrived at his flat that I thought to myself, My God, what are you doing here? I was only nineteen and fairly green. I had come straight from ballet training college into the world of light entertainment. And there I was, alone in a bachelor's apartment.

'The interview must have gone well. I was invited back, and on my return visit we had a very pleasant lunch. But the first interview was a much more business-like affair. Girls were arriving every fifteen minutes or so. He encouraged me to sing, and would strum along on a guitar as accompaniment. He was testing for voice and personality. Dialects were also something he wanted to test me on. Good looks were important, but not the only ticket needed to get into Benny's shows. He was far keener on enthusiasm. The wanting to participate.'

Once a girl was part of the team the future was fairly bright and promising. 'But sometimes Benny realised he'd made an error. Maybe there would be a personality clash with someone. More likely someone trying to tell him how to do his show. That's impossible, as it's Benny's "baby" from start to finish. He likes ideas,

ABOVE: **As an improbable 'bunny'.**
RIGHT: **Little Jackie Wright**, as usual getting the dome of his head slapped by the comedian.
BELOW: Benny loses to a 'one-armed bandit'.

RIGHT: **Benny relaxing as Fred Scuttle.**
BELOW: **Benny relaxing over a drink.**

Benny updates his
cop image (see p. 88–
89) to portray both
Cagney and Lacey

OVERLEAF: With
Jenny Lee-Wright
(left) and Louise
English.

Benny goes
international in
various guises.

Benny as himself for once. RIGHT: with Sue Upton's children Richard and Louise.

Scaling a studio prop
to great effect.

but the basic concept of how he sees it coming together is his not to be tampered with.

'I once made the error of fighting him over a routine in which he wanted me to wear a bikini. My argument was that there was a score of girls younger than me on the show, and with far better figures. I wouldn't give in, and I think that frustrated him. We laughed it off in the end, thankfully. He said to me, referring to my remark about being overweight, "We both need our mouths clamped up because we eat too much."'

Choreographer Libby Roberts said, 'Benny likes to keep you on your toes. You don't know for sure if you're booked until the last minute, and you daren't ask in case he says no. It's not easy for the girls on this understanding. They get offers for other work, but are reluctant to accept unless Benny definitely doesn't want to use them. I've had to push him to make a quick decision on a few occasions. But, in fact, he doesn't forget you, how ever many are the years that pass without contact being made.'

Benny has often been accused of sexism, because of the use of semi-clad girls in his shows.

'He goes for a cleaner image now,' says Libby. 'Not so many scanty outfits. The sexist accusations deeply hurt him. But the shift of emphasis is very plain in the more recent productions.'

In the latest shows, as well as many, many others, is one of his closest friends, Sue Upton. Sue has worked with Benny for over twelve years. Like most other girls,

Full cycle: the girls are
wearing clothes
again. Behind Benny
is Thames star
Dennis Waterman of
Minder fame.

she went through the auditioning ritual, and she, too, knows about the sexism accusations.

'There are those who say how disgusting it is that he should run around at the end of each show chasing half-naked girls. "They should look again," he once said to me. "It's the girls chasing *me*." And he's quite right, for fundamentally he has cast himself as the hapless clown.'

Discovering that Sue was clearly talented, Benny decided to offer her a more substantial role in the show.

'I was fully made-up one day,' she

Sue Upton, highly convincing as an old lady, combats the forces of evil . . .

68

recalled. 'He said to me, "You know, you've a lovely little pert face. I can just picture you dressed up as some funny old woman."

'We did a sketch where an old lady – me – crosses the road, is narrowly missed by a passing car, then gets bonked on the head by a belisha beacon. It worked well, and overnight I became an old lady.'

They have formed a special friendship. Benny stays with her and her family from time to time, and has had occasion to use her two children, Richard and Louise, in his shows.

The first time he visited her, the house was undergoing an extension. 'We were in a right mess, virtually living in the dining-room. I jokingly told him that there was much work to do on the place, and that it

In his mid-sixties, Benny has a cuddly, granddad quality about him.

was all right for him, money was no object. It was a bit careless of me really. It embarrassed him a bit. I didn't mean to, of course. Fortunately, he is *so* well off that it makes it more amusing than embarrassing to recall now.'

Benny is a keen walker, and Sue would take him and the kids down to Southend-on-Sea, where they could walk long stretches of beach.

'He would watch Richard and Louise, laughing and pointing at their antics, while I'd be making him eat chips out of a bag, telling him it was the right thing to do when at the coast.

'Then afterwards he would buy a load of sweets saying, "One for Richard, one for Louise and one for Benny." And he would see me teasingly scowling out the corner of his eye – he has such a sweet tooth. "And what about you, fatty?" he'd smile.'

Sue sometimes feels that because of their friendship, her family has become a substitute for the one Benny never had. 'Benny's a bachelor. He's lived alone for years. He lights up when he visits the kids, and never forgets their birthdays.

'One week when he was staying, he insisted on coming to playschool with me to collect Richard. I told him he could stay in the car. I always choose to play it down when he's around. He comes to relax, not to be put on show for the neighbourhood. "No, no, it's all right," he assured me, climbing out the car. And he followed me right inside, talking to the teachers, parents and kids.

'They were pleasantly surprised. This

was an unexpected side of Benny. In a way, I'm sure he wanted to go through the experience for the sake of the experience itself: to see what it feels like to be a dad, collecting his kid from school. Anything we consider everyday or mundane, he is intrigued by. And he has to be reasonably curious to put up with staying with us when you have Richard banging on the bathroom door saying, "Hurry up, Benny! I want to do a wee!"'

In his mid-sixties, Benny, it appears, has the cuddly, granddad quality about him. 'When I gave birth to Richard, Benny came across London to Romford, to visit me in hospital. Not driving a car made the whole effort all the greater. I felt very honoured that he should care so much.'

Benny with the children of girls who've worked on the show.

BENNY was once a fanatical traveller. He still makes regular visits to Europe, but they are not as carefree as they used to be. 'There was a time when he would literally sit at a table in a Paris street café, or wherever, scribbling notes on the back of a well-worn menu card,' remembered Philip Jones. 'He's too recognisable now. The quiet table in the quiet European street no longer exists for him.'

Knowing Benny to be so popular, it is easy to understand why travel is increasingly difficult for him.

A while ago, somebody wrote in the *Daily Mirror* that they had heard roars of laughter escaping from a backroom in a taverna, located in some tranquil Sicilian hamlet. When the person in question inves-

Not quite the kind of medical attention most of us receive.

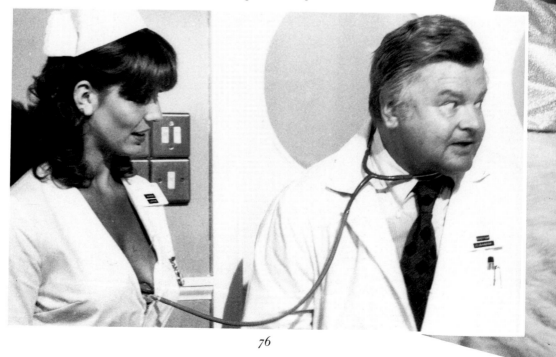

tigated, they were amazed to discover the entire family – granny and all – grouped around a small television set, intensely watching Benny Hill sprinting in and out of bushes, hotly pursued by nubile netball players, nurses and traffic wardens. There is hardly a place left in the world where he can remain unrecognised.

Henry McGee was in Canada, some years ago. 'A German gentleman approached me, recognising me from the show. Benny, as fans will know, does what we consider to be a very passable impression of a German. This gentleman took me solicitously to one side, and asked me with all sincerity, and in a strong accent, "This Beeny Heel! Is it true he is really German?"'

Bob Todd has had a similar experience. 'I was staying in a hotel in Hamburg. I went to a nearby bar, and a hulking German with all the bearing of an SS officer came bounding in. Big-shouldered, cropped hair, narrow-eyed. He was quite awesome. During the war I'd bombed Hamburg about thirty times. I began thinking this was my come-uppance. He sat across the bar giving me questioning glances.

'After a time, he moved next to me. "You vant von of those?" he asked, pointing at my glass. Having a quick re-think, I now decided he was a poof. But no. He moved so close to me I could feel his breath on my face. Then, in a lowered voice he said, "*Benny Hill Show,* ja!" I thought this a prelude to being hit. But then he suddenly clapped his hands against his thighs several times, letting out a broken, raucous laugh.

"Benny Heel! Benny Heel! Very, very funny."'

With the shows now transmitted world-wide, Bob and Henry suffer the recognition problem that Benny himself does.

'What usually happens,' said Bob, 'is that you get recognised and then asked what is probably the most asked question ever. "But what's he really like?" I always maintain he's a very nice bloke. But that's not enough, naturally. It's not what they're after. "Yes, but what's he *really* like?" they persist. Sometimes I'm tempted to go to the other extreme. "Oh, Benny Hill! Well, he's in prison, you know. What for? Oh, he's homosexual. Likes dressing up as women. And there's the whipping. He's into all that."

'And sometimes you want to say, "He's an effing bastard." Anything, other than the truth, because the truth, as is often the case, is mundane.'

But recognition can be quite amusing, as Bob discovered one morning outside the Piccadilly Hotel, London.

He was approached by two American ladies, both the other side of middle-age by some way, and with blue rinsed hair.

'"Er, pardon me," said one, the accent as whiney as you could imagine, "but aren't you the ... No. No, you can't be ..."

'"It is," squeaked her friend. "You ask 'im. You're Barb Tard, aren't you?"

'"Oh my God, it is. Just stay right there."

'She calls over a third woman. "Hey, look who it is from the *Benny Hill Show* ..." And so it went on.'

Looking like an important traveller.

81

No-one connected with Benny, though, quite suffers the recognition problem to the extent of the man himself.

Benny got off a tram at a wrong stop late one night when on a visit to Hong Kong. It transpired he had stumbled into the red light district. All the bartenders and whores went wild when they recognised him, and they had a spontaneous party. They knew him very well because his shows went out at 3.30 in the morning there, which was about the time whores, bar and club people knocked off.

Being Benny's producer for so many years has meant a great friendship has developed between Dennis Kirkland and the comedian, one that goes beyond the confines of work.

En route to Greece with Dennis Kirkland.

With such a friendship there inevitably come the amusing anecdotes. One such anecdote points out the minus side of owning one of the most instantly recognisable faces on the planet.

Dennis and Benny took two girls from the show – intentions being strictly honourable – on a short trip to Athens. The idea was to get a break from the abortive English weather. (They were to arrive in pouring rain, having been informed that in England a sudden heatwave had just set in.)

During the flight over they relaxed with a few drinks, and generally anticipated the warmth and tranquillity that lay ahead.

On the aircraft, Benny was one side of the aisle with a Hill's Angel, Dennis the other.

'I sent a note across to him,' Dennis recalled. '"Stop getting pissed!" it said. "I'm not," he mouthed back with a smile.

'Then, more seriously, I reminded him that when we arrived we were to go straight to the First Class lounge and do an interview that we'd promised to do for them. "So comb your hair," I added. I'm very fatherly at times with him, though no doubt he'll smack me in the gob one of these days.'

The plane landed and began taxiing towards the disembarkation area.

Dennis happened to glance through his window as they came smoothly to a halt and heard the engines shutting off.

'"Effing hell!" was my initial reaction,' said Dennis. 'There was a barrage of photographers and pressmen numbering somewhere between fifty and sixty strong, all

Benny's genius for impersonation goes beyond mere disguise – he masters posture and mannerisms with apparent ease

on the apron waiting for Benny to emerge. I called to him in a weak voice.

'"What's up?" he asked, puzzled. "Take a look out there," I told him. He was jolted. This was all totally unexpected. We had only agreed to do a little interview in the privacy of the lounge, not an impromptu on the tarmac.'

Dennis went to see the Captain, returning with his flight cap which he gave to Benny. Benny stood on the metal steps at the doorway to the plane, the hat on his head tilted to one side as in the pose of his famous Fred Scuttle character.

It appealed to them, but eventually Dennis had to get Benny moved to the right place if only to let the aircraft return to London.

'But the Greeks don't really care too much about protocol,' recollected Dennis. 'They bashed each other about with no semblance of respect or dignity. All they wanted was their photo or interview. All other considerations were immaterial. It was a nightmare.'

He did manage at last to free Benny, and get them a space on the courtesy bus.

'But then an official comes on board,' went on Dennis. 'She takes Benny and me off the bus and into a waiting, gleaming limousine. This is to travel a distance all of one hundred yards to the terminal building. A bit perplexing.'

The lounge was in a state of chaos, but the interview went ahead. Dennis jokingly asked someone if the pandemonium was going to haunt them the whole time they were staying in Athens. With a straight face he was told, Yes.

"ARR

Two interpretations of the Fred Scuttle character.

A police escort took their small group to their hotel in the centre of Athens. Their driver, who was a self-confessed Benny Hill maniac, also drove like one.

'He hardly stayed on the road,' sighed Dennis. 'We all went as white as a sheet, and it can't have done one of the girls – Emma – much good. She was pregnant at the time.'

It had been arranged that their first few days would be free of any commitments. Then after that, Benny would do any number of photo calls they wanted of him.

The first afternoon they found a peaceful square, and Benny and Dennis sat down to have a beer while the girls went off shopping. But it wasn't to remain peaceful.

'All the traffic passing around the square began to slow down, in the end causing a major traffic jam. "Any Eel!" they began telling each other. "Look! Any Eel!" That's

something how they pronounce his name out there.

'They started waving and laughing and hooting their horns. The police arrived to see what was going on, and when a bus joined the jam, the passengers began getting off to have a better look. "Shall we move on?" whispered Benny, calmly sipping his beer. "Don't think that's possible, dear," I whispered back. "But try waving and we'll slowly retreat." This worked, and presumably the chaos gradually subsided.'

The first planned photo call was supposed to take place on the Acropolis.

Benny was to wear a special outfit for them while standing at this historical site.

'We never reached the top,' said Dennis. 'The taxi took us as far as it could, then

Benny doubles as Starsky and Hutch. Jackie Wright makes a brilliant Huggy Bear.

we got out and gazed with horror as all attention focused on Benny. American, French, German, British and Greek. They were all there.

'We made fifteen yards before a human wall of four hundred or more chanting tourists prevented us penetrating any further. "Ben-eee, Ben-eee," was the chant.

'An official there apologised, but said we would have to leave. We must have been the first people thrown off the Acropolis since the Turks.'

*N*OT only is Benny a very private man, but it can be said that, to a small degree, he is a touch eccentric. Of course, if we were all continuously under the scrutiny of the public eye, we might perhaps be considered eccentrics, too.

David Croft can recall that at one time during the early sixties, Benny's accounts were apparently out by some thirty thousand pounds. It was later discovered that he hadn't been cashing his cheques but stockpiling them in a drawer, such was his lack of enthusiasm regarding money.

His friend Peter Charlesworth still shakes his head with amused disbelief at some of Benny's antics.

'A few years ago, there came a newsflash on the radio saying "Benny Hill dying – seriously ill in London hospital."

'I urgently tracked him down to the Cromwell Clinic, where it transpired he was staying.

'I had expected to be put through to a doctor telling me, in a grave, dark voice, that it wouldn't be possible to speak with the patient. Instead, I was put directly through to Benny.

'"Oh, hello Peter," came his chirpy voice. I asked him if he was okay, and what had he gone in for. He told me he was having treatment carried out on an ulcer. No more, no less.

'I asked him why he'd been there a whole week. "I like it here," he answered. "It's very nice. Good room service, and plenty of peace and quiet."

Benny doesn't quite capture Noël Coward's *savoir faire.*

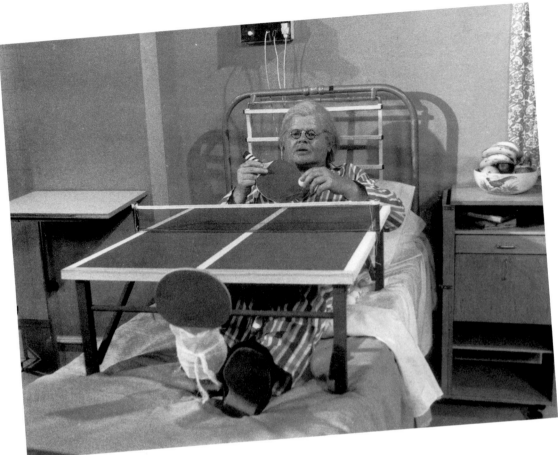

'Unbelievably, he'd stayed on there for an extra week because it was isolated and comfortable for him. He could pick and choose which calls to take as he was protected by a switchboard from the outside world, and just enjoy being waited on hand and foot. Not many people would actually choose to stay in hospital. And it must have cost him a packet.'

Peter regards himself as somewhat fortunate in having been able to glimpse Benny Hill, the man.

'He's extremely careful about relationships,' he pointed out. 'When you become a celebrity, you are put upon from all quarters. Benny made the fast and sensible decision to avoid all the gloss and concentrate all his efforts solely on making

Benny enjoys being in hospital.

his shows. No panel shows, chat shows, guest appearances et cetera. And any charity work he does is carried out as a private individual.'

Benny, it is true, formed a friendship with a disabled Felixstowe woman nearly forty years ago. He keeps in close contact with her, and spends one week a year at her home. There is another disabled woman in Leicestershire, who receives the same treatment.

A private man who likes to do his own shopping . . .

Benny brilliant in
drag again.

Peter commented, 'He's always been able to switch off when away from work. On top of this, he tends, if anything, to shy away from the celebrity image. I've never witnessed him playing the "big star" routine. He's always been himself, first, then a famous comedian. I think the press and public have probably concluded that there's no mileage in hounding him. That he likes to do his own shopping, the press,

More birthday celebrations. Sue Upton [far right of picture] looking somewhat younger than how she usually appears in the shows.

apparently, found quite extraordinary. A man of his wealth and position shouldn't do such things. It's nonsense, of course. He's a bachelor, and he enjoys shopping. So what? Benny definitely doesn't conform to the cliché role of a high profile millionaire. If that makes him appear a bit eccentric, then fair enough.'

Money itself seems to hold little value to Benny, as Peter, like David Croft, once discovered.

'He said to me, "All right, so I've got quite a bit of money. But I can't see it. It's just pieces of paper. If I had a room with a million pounds in it, I might just be a little more in awe of it all. But I haven't. So I'm not."'

PA for the late Ken Carter, who produced the earliest BBC shows – from the mid-fifties to early sixties – was Valerie Willis. She remembers Benny as a generous man.

'He would buy presents for people connected with the show. He would make a note of a certain perfume one of the make-up girls used, and at the end of the show he would bring her some of it.

'Once he approached me in front of lots of people with a present, hinting it was the right size for a large-breasted woman. He insisted I opened it in front of everyone. I was very embarrassed, but did as he asked. It was a beautiful shawl.'

He could also be generous with his time, as Valerie remembered. 'I was doing a trial course at producing *Blue Peter*. I asked Benny if he would do a short piece for me that tied in with children. Having his name associated to the show could only do me good. He said he would do it as a favour, but he didn't want the offer of payment. This was because, "You wouldn't be able to pay what I would ask." And so he did it – for nothing.'

Benny is a man of simple needs. His idea of entertainment can range from going out to a show and dinner, to a walk in the park – as Erica Lynley discovered.

'He took me to lunch in London, and afterwards we went shopping in Harrods.

BELOW: **Benny is a man of simple needs. His idea of entertainment can be no more than a walk in the park.**

OPPOSITE: **Willing the photographer away.**

He likes Harrods. Then we went to Hyde Park, sat down in deck-chairs and read newspapers, only speaking when we came across something of interest in print. How often, I've long wondered, do you go out with a famous star, and end up reading papers in the park? It's a very fond memory for me.'

David Croft remembers one of the few times he socialised with Benny, during the time he was producing his show in the mid-sixties. 'There were three of us planning to go out for dinner. Me, a friend and Benny.

With Peter Butterworth and Janet Brown at the Lakeside Country Club, celebrating the 'Club of the Year' Award.

We both had girlfriends at the time, but
Benny didn't. "Doesn't matter," he said,
casually producing an address book. He
dialled a number. "Hello Mary, it's sexy
here." A pause. "Oh, hello Mrs Smith, is
Mary there?"'

Sue Upton can recall the time Benny
took her to see a cabaret show at London's
Talk of the Town, this being long before
Stringfellow turned it into the Hippodrome.

'The singing duo Peters and Lee were
performing that night. But the audience

**Enjoying a tipple with
comedian Eric Sykes,
and Philip Jones.**

ABOVE, CENTRE: **Rich Burt and Eliza Tayl in** *Who's Afraid of Virgin Wool?* **The other pictures show a few of the many celebrity guests who have made surprise appearances on the shows.**

was more interested in Benny's arrival. Whispers got around that he was there, and heads began to turn. People stood up and started applauding. They were just delighted to see him in the flesh.

'It was my birthday treat to be going there. Benny was particularly exhausted that night from working, and half way through the evening he dozed off at the table, head resting in hands.

'Just at the moment I noticed this, I heard Peters and Lee, on stage, saying, "We're very pleased to inform you we have a famous personality among us tonight . . ." In a moment of panic, I kicked Benny under the table, his arms slipped away, his head fell forwards, and he awoke with a start and a grunt.

'"Quick!" I said to him. "Stand up and bow." That was just as they finished the announcement, ". . . Mr Benny Hill." Benny leaped up, wondering what on earth was happening, poor man.'

OTHER than travelling, Benny is not a hobbies man. 'He only has one hobby,' says Dennis Kirkland, with a smile. 'Eating! As far as Benny is concerned there is no such thing as bad food. If it is edible, then it is good. And he hates to leave anything on his plate. "Think of the poor starving who can't get food," he'll tell you. I've never been quite sure if he's serious about that one.'

Harold Snoad recalls visits in the early '60s to the Fulham home of Benny's then producer, Ken Carter.

'We used to go there to have work meetings – discussions about the shows. We would all be gathered around a table, then Benny would go missing. Invariably he could be found rifling through Ken's fridge having himself a snack. He'd never ask or say anything. Such was Benny's appetite.'

But Sue Upton adds that Benny does love television. 'He'll watch anything. He's particularly fond of nostalgia and sport. Boxing is a big thing with him. He tries never to miss a fight. I rang him up one morning after a Tyson fight, and we nattered on for ages all about it. Afterwards, I had to confess to him I wasn't really that up on it; not as much as I'd been purporting to be. I genned up because *he* was so keen. I like to make him feel I care; that I'm willing to make an effort. It would be very boring if you didn't try to converse about some of the things that interest him. And he laughed a lot after my confession about

the boxing.'

If Benny is a man of few hobbies, it doesn't appear to detract from his leading a full life. He wouldn't be able to travel as he does should he live a cluttered up existence. Being a single man with monetary freedom has given him the opportunities many do not have.

'A long time ago,' recalled Sue, 'he said to me, "It wouldn't be fair on someone having to put up with me." He likes to travel and he likes to write. His lifestyle wouldn't appeal to many. He is quite unique – extraordinary, even. He'll jot down notes wherever he may be.'

Benny's notes are something that can bring an immediate groan from long-suffering Dennis Kirkland. 'When he's

Benny as his Chinese character, Chow Mein.

Hapless Benny shelters Jenny Lee-Wright.

travelling he doesn't take note paper with him. The whole of the first routine in which he introduced us all to his Chinese character who says things wrongly, and invariably crudely, came back to us at Thames on a cardboard slip taken from a shirt he'd had laundered at a hotel. No-one at the office could understand what it was about. You see, he never mentioned that it was supposed to be a Chinaman. Instead, we found ourselves wrestling with phrases like "Stewpit gay iriot"!'

Benny is clearly unpretentious. His attitude to people is as unaffected as his attitude to all the things that make up his life. And as Sue Upton said, 'I have always stated that he would be just as happy having dinner with the check-out girl at Sainsbury's as any celebrated figure.'

Henry McGee sees him as a man with genuine humility. 'One day, two or three years ago, there was a fabulous article that appeared on Benny in the *Evening Standard*,' recollected Henry. 'It's rare for any artiste to receive such written praise. It was all about what a clever man he was, and how loved he was by those around him. I happened to have a copy with me in the rehearsal room.

'"Benny!" I called over to him. "Have you seen this? It's marvellous."

'"Oh, er, yes," he replied, almost sheepishly. "I heard something about it."

'"You couldn't have written it better yourself."

'"Oh, really," came the unexcited response.

'He mentioned something about reading it later on, but I know he won't have done. He doesn't want to be a part of that side of the business. What people have to say about him in an analytical way doesn't interest him. He would choose rather to ignore it. There are few people who would so under-react to being told they are the best thing since walking on the water.'

Benny has achieved so much that there can be little pressure on him once away from the studios.

Philip Jones has witnessed the growth of a legend. 'It is clear to me,' he said thoughtfully, 'that Benny is unaffected by his success, arguably more so than any other artiste in his field I've either known or met. And also, the respect shown to him by his peers has grown in direct proportion to his success. I've seen the evaluation of him go from, "Well, it's just a crumpet show, isn't it?" to "My God, how unbelievable and marvellous are his achievements."'

*I*T would be wrong to think that success has turned Benny into a recluse, as the British press would have us believe.

'Benny is not so much a recluse,' revealed Peter Charlesworth, 'as a man able to isolate himself. He's the only human being I think I have come across who needs no other human company. He enjoys solitude. He cooks – very well – he potters about, he watches television. Sure, he has friends and enjoys company, but only on his own terms, for he is equally content on his own.

'In America, they cannot understand that a star of his calibre doesn't want the glitz and razzmatazz – that, in fact, he shuns it. They think you're kidding them if you tell them that he lives alone in a modest house on the south coast of England.'

Peter added seriously, 'But if you are a friend of Benny's, then you are a friend for life, though he does not keep up relationships as most other people do. He doesn't ring every week, sometimes not for months, even. Then he'll phone, and talk and talk, and you'll go out and have a meal together, and then you won't see or hear from him again for about another six months. But he's nobody's fool. If you think he is, and try to take advantage, that's when he'll rear up. You take a liberty with Benny, and that's the end of the friendship.'

Henry McGee remarked upon his temperament. 'He has the most equable temperament imaginable. He doesn't appear to get annoyed or irate about things. He never raises his voice to you, even if there's a good deal of tension there. Extraordinary, really. He's such a self-contained man. Meeting him coming out of his dressing room for the very first time all those years back, is like meeting him today. He hasn't changed at all.'

Nicholas Parsons recalls:

'I invited him to a party some years ago, not realising then that he didn't like to go to that kind of thing. More remarkable therefore that he should have accepted. He often mentions it to me, saying, "That was a lovely party. Not too theatrical." You see, Benny doesn't want to talk about Benny. He likes to meet – to see – other types of people.

'I once pointed out to Benny that he had handled his career just right. I said, "You only work five or so months of the year actually doing the shows, giving yourself time to write and travel and study for future shows. Most comedians are obsessional about work. They can't stop. Week in week out." This interested him. "I'd never thought about it like that," he said. Thinking about it, he could see that doing less had in a way given him more.'

There seems to be little more to add about Britain's most successful comedian. He has mastered several languages – fluent in French, German and Spanish – and for the sake of a new routine long ago, one that was destined to become his brass bandsman character, Fred Scuttle, he learned to play cornet.

He has studied many styles of music

including Latin American, and as well as playing guitar and cornet, he is accomplished on the Paraguayan harp.

As Peter Charlesworth remarked, 'He has great concentration, and a mind that picks up sounds very easily.'

I leave the final word to Bob Todd, whose closing comment summed up what many people I have met during the compiling of this book have implied.

'If you took time to consider all the hugely wealthy and successful stars there are in this world, you would be hard pushed to find one as nice and as normal as Benny Hill. It sounds like hero-worship, but is, in fact, the truth.'